# EXPERIMENTING WITH
# WITH
# AIR AND FLIGHT

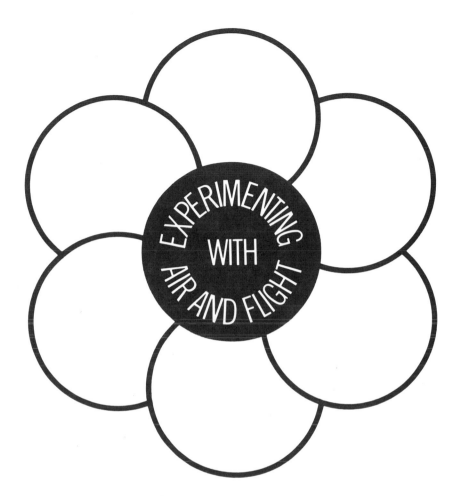

EXPERIMENTING WITH AIR AND FLIGHT

# BY ORMISTON H. WALKER

ILLUSTRATED BY ANNE CANEVARI GREEN
FRANKLIN WATTS 1989
NEW YORK LONDON TORONTO SYDNEY
A VENTURE BOOK

Photographs courtesy of: The Granger Collection: p. 10;
Photo Researchers: pp. 23 (Phil Farnes), 42 (top, Steve
Krasemann); British Airways: p. 26; Bettmann Archive:
pp. 35, 59, 74; Peter Arnold: p. 42 (bottom, Steve Krasemann); General Dynamics Corporation: p. 52; U.S. Navy:
pp. 66, 72; NASA: p. 81.

Library of Congress Cataloging-in-Publication Data

Walker, Ormiston H.
    Experimenting with air and flight / Ormiston H.
Walker;
    illustrated by Anne Canevari Green.
        p.    cm.—(A Venture book)
    Bibliography: p.
    Includes index.
    Summary: Suggests experiments and projects to dem-
onstrate the properties of air and the mechanics of flight by
such objects as airplanes, balloons, and kites.
    ISBN 0-531-10670-5
    1. Flight—Experiments—Juvenile literature.
[1. Flight -Experiments. 2. Experiments.]
I. Green, Anne Canevari, ill. II. Title.
TL547.W24    1989
629.13—dc19                    88-38063    CIP    AC

# CONTENTS

*The author wishes to thank
Maurice Seay, aeronautical engineer,
and Peers Seed, electronic engineer,
for reading the manuscript, and for
helpful advice and suggestions.*

# EXPERIMENTING WITH
# AIR AND FLIGHT

# A SHORT HISTORY OF FLIGHT

Our dreams of flight are as old as history. Ancient legends and religions tell of gods and heroes who flew. Mercury was the winged messenger of the Greek gods. The winged horse Pegasus carried the Greek hero Bellerophon into battle on its back. The mythical Greeks Daedalus and Icarus built wings of feathers and wax in their attempt to fly.

The ancient Chinese, too, were interested in flight. They experimented with rockets and kites. Cultures in China as well as in the Middle East and the Americas had legends about gods in flying chariots.

In the fifteenth century, the great artist and inventor Leonardo da

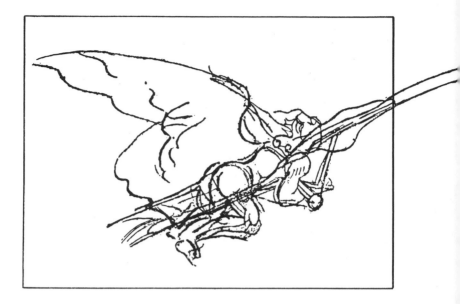

**Leonardo da Vinci's drawing of
an ornithopter, with the pilot's
legs moving together and the wings
hand-operated on the upstroke**

Vinci designed machines called ornithopters in which
a human being was supposed to become airborne by
flapping his wings. Unfortunately the machines never
flew because the "motor" was too weak.

In the eighteenth century, the Montgolfier brothers in France launched their first hot-air balloon. The
balloon was made of linen and paper buttoned together in sections, and the hot air came from burning
straw.

Orville and Wilbur Wright built and flew the first
powered aircraft in 1903.

In the years since the Wright brothers' historic flight, air travel and airplanes have changed enormously. Today, air travel is an accepted part of our lives, and airplanes move faster than the Wright brothers could have dreamed possible. And of course we now are able to travel to the moon and send space probes to the distant planets.

Yet despite our progress, we still have a long way to go before we match the flying ability of birds and insects. And although we have built machines to enable us to fly like birds and insects, we cannot fly unaided.

This book is designed to help you better understand the nature and mysteries of flight. Through experiments and projects you will explore the properties of air and the mechanics of airplanes, balloons, and kites. Perhaps you will come up with some new ways of doing things to enlarge our understanding of flight or improve the technology of flight.

# KEEPING ALOFT

Air is all around us. We can feel air moving in and out of our bodies when we breathe. Although we can neither smell nor taste air, we can feel it moving past us. Air moves slowly in a gentle breeze and fast in a strong wind. Gentle winds stir up autumn leaves; strong winds can uproot trees; hurricanes can destroy buildings. Air can move up, down, and sideways. In a hurricane, air can even move in circles or spirals.

We know that air can hold up kites, balloons, and airplanes. But although we feel air and can measure certain things about air—including temperature, speed, and moisture content—can we prove that air exists? After all, scientists shouldn't make assumptions, even about the most obvious things.

So before learning about flight, perhaps we should learn a little about air—that is, if it really exists.

**IS AIR REAL?** • Have an adult help you punch six to twelve holes with a nail or awl in the bottom of a plastic container like a soft-drink or seltzer bottle. Lower the container into a bucket, pot, or sink full of water for a minute or two (see figure 1). Lift out the bottle. What happens?

Lower the container into the water again. Press your hand or thumb firmly over the top and lift the container out. What happens this time?

Now place your hand or thumb over the top and lower the bottle into the water once again. What do you observe?

The ancient Greek doctor Empedocles performed similar experiments in 450 B.C. using a ladle with holes in the base and an open tube on top. When he lowered the device into water and then took it out, top open, the water ran out, making a small shower. But if he kept his thumb over the top when he removed the device, the water stayed in it until he raised his thumb. When he tried to fill the ladle with his thumb over the top, nothing happened.

Although Empedocles saw no substance blocking the way, he assumed that air was blocking the water. "Air," said Empedocles, "is matter made up of such tiny particles that we cannot see them." Air exerted pressure against the water, preventing it from flowing out of the ladle.

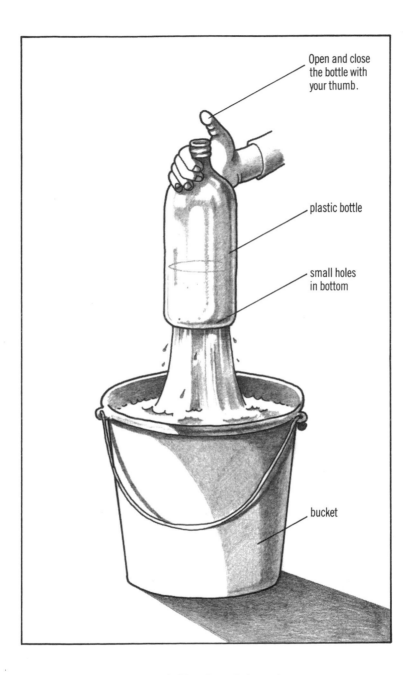

Open and close the bottle with your thumb.

plastic bottle

small holes in bottom

bucket

**Figure 1. Showing air is real.**

Have you assured yourself that air is real? If you are not yet convinced, you might try some additional experiments. Put one finger over the nozzle of a bicycle pump and try to work the pump. What do you find? Pump up a tire. Do you hear anything in the tire? If air isn't real, what has caused the tire to inflate? When you are riding your bike, why don't the tires flatten beneath your weight?

**AIR PRESSURE AND THE POWER OF AIR** • Air may exist, but how can air, which is so light, support a huge airplane? During a storm, how can moving air (wind) make the ride so bumpy?

Use a measuring cup with a lip to pour about a cupful (¼ liter) of hot tap water into a 1-quart (1-liter) screwtop plastic bottle. BE CAREFUL NOT TO BURN YOURSELF. If you have a funnel, you can use it to simplify your job.

Wear an oven mitt and hold a thick cloth over the mouth of the bottle and shake the bottle well. Quickly replace the cap, turning it firmly. What happens to the bottle as it cools?

Air, though invisible, is a real substance. It has weight and can push. Still, it's one thing for air to push in the sides of a soda bottle and another to hold up a 27,000-pound (12,000 kg) airplane! In other words, how can air pressure support a heavy airplane?

**LIFT** • To answer this question, you might start with the following simple experiment.

Hold a sheet of notebook paper with its near end curled over your forefingers, as shown in figure 2.

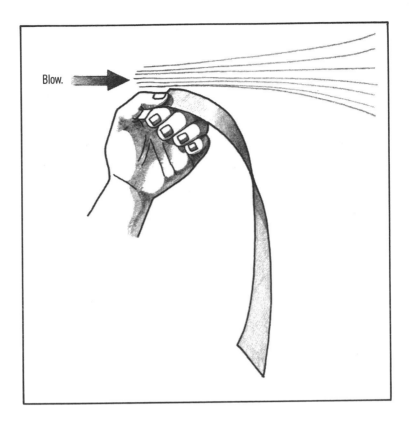

Blow.

Figure 2. Air pressure and lift.

Hold the paper about 1 inch (2.5 cm) from your mouth. If you were to blow strongly below the sheet, then strongly above it, which airstream, upper or lower, would raise the paper higher? Now try the experiment. Are you surprised by the result? Try the experiment again.

What is going on? When you make a rapid airstream you also produce low pressure in the stream. The harder you blow, the faster the airstream, the less the pressure above the paper, and the more strongly the atmosphere below the paper can push it up. Although blowing against the underside of the paper also lifts the paper up, blowing on the top is more effective.

When an airplane builds up speed on the ground, the air flowing over the top of the wings create a zone of very low pressure. The force of the atmosphere beneath the wings pushes up on the wings, causing the plane to take off when the speed is high enough and the pressure low enough. The force of the air on the plane is called *lift*.

You can demonstrate how an airstream produces lift on a model wing of your own design. Fold a sheet of writing paper to form a smooth, curving bend. Use cellophane tape to form a wing from the two free edges, as shown in figure 3. Tape the wing to one end of a yardstick or meterstick and balance using a loop of string. Blow through a piece of rubber tubing or a flexible straw so that the airstream flows across the upper wing surface. What happens to the wing?

**WING SHAPES** • Theoretically, wings could be made in all sizes and shapes. But in fact, wings usually have a curved upper surface. Why is this so?

AIRSTREAMS AND FLAT SURFACES ○ First let's investigate the interaction between air and flat surfaces.

Cut a piece of writing paper 4 × 8 inches (10 × 20 cm) and bend it down 1 inch (2.5 cm) at the short ends to form a bridge. Put the "bridge" on a table.

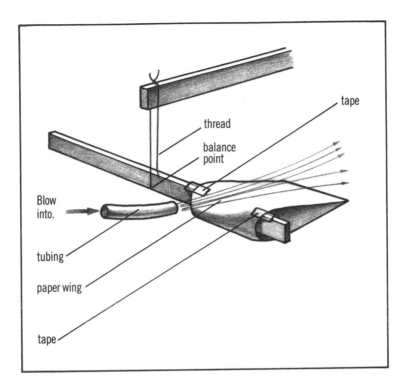

**Figure 3. Airstreams and wing curves.**

Blow hard under the bridge and note what happens. Cut a 2-inch (5-cm) square of light cardboard. Put a straight pin through the center and put the card over an empty thread spool with the pin sticking in the hole in the spool.

Hold your head back and try to blow the card off the reel. While blowing through the spool, bend forward and downward. What happens? What happens when you run out of breath?

Blow between two sheets of newspaper held a few inches (or cm) apart and note what happens. Can you explain your findings?

AIRSTREAMS AND CURVED SURFACES ∘ Now let's investigate the effects of air on curved surfaces.

1. Hang two small empty cans about 2 inches (5 cm) apart from a clamp-and-stand setup or from the top of a doorway. Blow between the cans. What happens? The cans have curved surfaces like an airplane wing.

2. Place a new Ping-Pong ball in a funnel. Blow hard through the funnel. Can you dislodge the ball? Blow harder. What happens? The rapid airstream produces low pressure between the side of the ball (a curved surface like an airplane wing) and the inside of the funnel. With the ball in the funnel, quickly turn the funnel upside down while blowing in the narrow end. Can you prevent the ball from dropping out of the funnel?

Because the top surface of a wing is curved, it is longer than the bottom surface. Air flowing over the top surface moves faster than over the bottom surface. Since faster air creates lower pressure, more lift is generated. The curvature is called *camber*.

Engineers refer to wings as airfoils—objects that generate lift under certain conditions. Figure 4 shows an airfoil in action. Experiment with the shapes shown in figure 5. Make a handle by taping the shapes to a pencil or stick at one end as shown in the

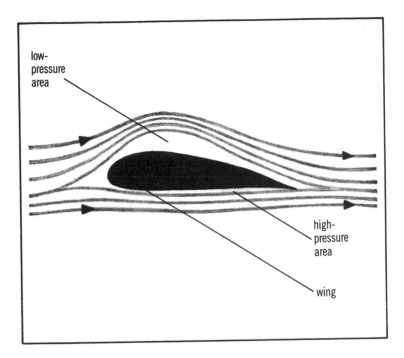

low-pressure area

high-pressure area

wing

Figure 4. A wing in moving air.

figure. Try the different shapes outside in a wind. Which has the most lift? Look at photographs of airplanes in books. Study the different wing shapes and sizes. Build some wings shaped like those you see. Which work best? Design your own wing shapes and experiment with different sizes.

**OUTDOOR OBSERVATIONS** • As an aeronautical engineer (someone who designs airplanes), you will find it instructive to study birds in flight.

Do all birds fly the same way? Do some flap their

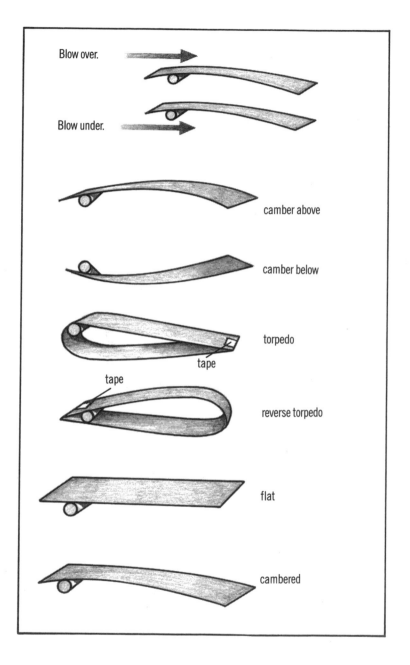

**Figure 5. Different wing shapes.**

**A red-tailed hawk in flight**

wings a lot while others seem to soar effortlessly?
Study wing shapes and sizes. Is there any connection
between wing size and shape and overall body size?
Is there a connection between wing size and shape
and flying habits? Do big birds like crows and gulls
do a lot of soaring? How do small birds like finches
fly? Can you find any swifts or swallows?

Watch birds like gulls and ducks close up. Does
the shape of their body suit their dual life in water
and in the air? When gulls and ducks take off, do
they fly into or away from the wind? Do they use
their tail and wings when landing?

Also observe insects such as dragonflies and butterflies, and watch fish. In a good aquarium you can examine the fins of all kinds of fish and other aquatic animals. Do fin shapes seem to follow the same rules you have learned about wing shapes in birds and airplanes?

Try to spot some predatory birds such as hawks and vultures. Do they seem to follow invisible airstreams? Find a place where people fly sailplanes (gliders) or hang gliders. Do the pilots also seem to be following air currents? Large upward air movements are called *thermals*. Do a little reading on thermals or talk to some sailplane enthusiasts.

In talking to these enthusiasts or to people who fly small planes for fun, you may encounter people with some of the same feelings that people have felt for thousands of years when they talk about flying like the birds.

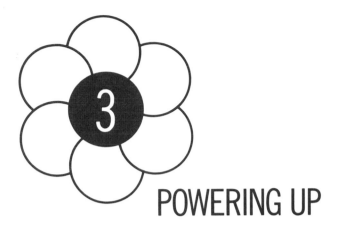

# POWERING UP

As you now know, the lifting force needed to hold a bird or aircraft aloft comes from a moving airstream flowing smoothly over its wings. To generate the moving airstream, there has to be another force that thrusts the bird or aircraft forward. A bird usually produces this force by flapping its wings, though once in the air a bird can often rely on wind or thermals to create the lift. An airplane, on the other hand, needs an engine to produce *thrust*—the force necessary both to get it into the air and then to keep it in the air.

All of this sounds easy enough, but things get more complicated once the plane begins moving. For one thing, resistance from the moving air—called *drag*—slows down the plane. For another, the force of *gravity* is constantly pulling down on the plane. The plane must move fast enough to create enough lift to overcome the downward force of gravity and the slowing force of drag.

Four forces are therefore at work on a moving airplane: lift, thrust, drag, and gravity (see figure 6). If you look at different airplane designs, you will find that each addresses the four forces in a different way, depending on the type of airplane.

**DRAG AND STREAMLINING** • For a plane to fly efficiently, the effects of drag must be minimized.

The Concorde, the world's first supersonic passenger plane, successfully addresses the four forces at work on a moving airplane: lift, thrust, drag, and gravity.

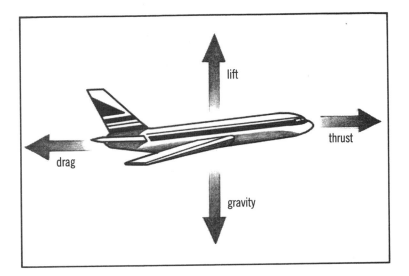

**Figure 6. Forces on an aircraft in flight.**

Drag has several components. One is air friction. Another is an uneven movement of air called *turbulence*. To minimize drag and create a smooth airflow, the bodies of many birds and aircraft are streamlined—rounded, tapering, narrowing at the nose and tail. The lines used to show how air flows around airfoils are called *streamlines*. Figure 7A shows streamlines. Figure 7B shows what happens when air hits a flat surface. The turbulence takes the form of swirls called eddies which create drag.

You also can see streamlining in the designs of racing cars, the helmets of racing cyclists, many fish, and the bodies of competitive swimmers.

To learn more about drag, try the following simple experiments.

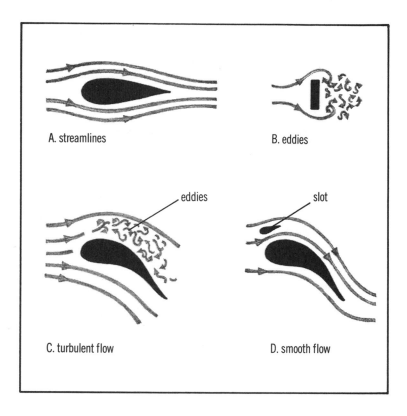

A. streamlines

B. eddies

eddies

slot

C. turbulent flow

D. smooth flow

**Figure 7. Streamlines and turbulence.**

Cut a piece of cardboard 3 × 6 inches (7.5 × 15 cm). Move the narrower edge just above the surface of the water in a tub. Repeat with the edge of the cardboard just beneath the surface of the water. What differences do you observe? Repeat these two actions using the wider edge of the cardboard and note the results.

On a windy day, hold a piece of cardboard 20 × 30 inches (50 × 75 cm) so that the wind blows against the flat side. Now hold the cardboard with the edge facing the wind. In which case is the drag greatest? Do you see any connection between surface area and drag? Experiment with different sizes of cardboard. Fold the cardboard into different shapes and experiment until you find a shape that resembles a plane and seems to offer the least resistance to the wind.

To learn more about turbulence, you may wish to try the following experiments. DO THEM UNDER ADULT SUPERVISION.

Cut a 2-inch (5-cm) square from a piece of light cardboard. Hold the card about 2 inches (5 cm) in front of a burning candle and about 4 inches (10 cm) from you, as shown in figure 8A. Blow hard against the card and observe the movement of the flame. Can you see any unusual movements of the flame? If so, you are observing turbulence.

Now take a piece of paper 2 × 4 inches (5 × 10 cm) and fold it into the shape of a wing, as shown in figure 8B. Do the same thing with the wing that you did with the card. What happens?

Experiment with other shapes until you find the shape that disturbs the flame the most evenly. Draw the streamlines. Also experiment with other objects, such as an apple, half an apple, a vase, a bottle.

**FINDING THE BEST SHAPE** • "An aircraft that creates minimal drag will fly smoothly." The same goes for any moving object, from footballs to Frisbees. Experiment with these and other objects until you feel convinced of the statement. Then try the following.

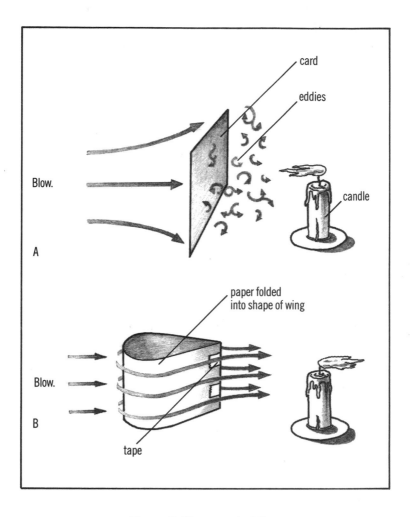

**Figure 8. Shape and airflow.**

Take a sheet of writing paper, carefully stand on a chair or at the top of a flight of stairs, hold the paper as high as you can, and release it. Then roll the paper into a ball and release as before. Which took the least time to reach the ground?

Here's another experiment: Wet your hand and let some drops of water fall into a sink while watching them against light from a window. Sketch the shapes the drops take as they fall. Also try oil and glycerine if you have some.

One last experiment will help you understand something about the relationship between shape and movement. Take two lumps of modeling clay. Form one into a flat disk and the other into a torpedo shape. Hold them over a large, wide-mouthed jar or over a sink or tub filled with water. Release them, flat side down for the disk and end down for the torpedo. Which hits bottom first?

If you have a chance to watch a track meet or practice, keep an eye on the discus thrower. Look at spaceships in science fiction movies. Why do some have wings and others not? How do flying saucers work? Experiment with paper plates of different sizes. Do they fly as well as a Frisbee or move as smoothly as a flat stone? Do some reading to see whether anyone has ever built a flying saucer that works.

**THRUST** • Thrust is the force that pushes an aircraft forward. A simple experiment will help you see this. Stand on a skateboard or put on a pair of skates. (Be careful!) Have an adult stand behind you to catch you if you slip. Hold a heavy schoolbag and toss it away from you. You will move in the opposite direction from the bag, so be prepared. What happens?

In a propeller-driven plane, a propeller does the pushing. In a jet, hot gases do the pushing. In both cases, Newton's third law of motion is at work: For every action, there is an equal and opposite reaction. A rocket works much the way a jet does.

Propeller aircraft work only up to a certain altitude. At a certain point the air is too thin for the propeller to grab onto. Jets, which can go much faster than propeller aircraft, work better at higher altitudes because of the reduced air friction. However, at a certain point there is not enough oxygen to burn the fuel. At this point you need a rocket, since a rocket ship carries its own supply of oxygen to burn the fuel.

**PROPELLERS AND HELICOPTERS** • A propeller threads its way through the air. An aircraft propeller can be thought of as a windmill threshing the air. A propeller with a cambered—slightly arched—shape works best, with the cambered surface facing the airstream, as shown in figure 9.

You can buy a model plane propeller or make your own from balsa wood. If you make your own propellers, sand some smooth and leave others rough. Make some with camber and others flat. You will not have this option with commercial plastic propellers. Instead, use rough sandpaper to roughen the blades of some of the plastic propellers.

To set the propellers spinning, build the helicopter mount shown in figure 10. BE SURE TO DO THIS EXPERIMENT OUTSIDE. Hold the launcher over your head and point the propeller away from yourself and other people in the area. Do a number of launches with each propeller straight up in still air and find the one that climbs highest. Do the several tests with each

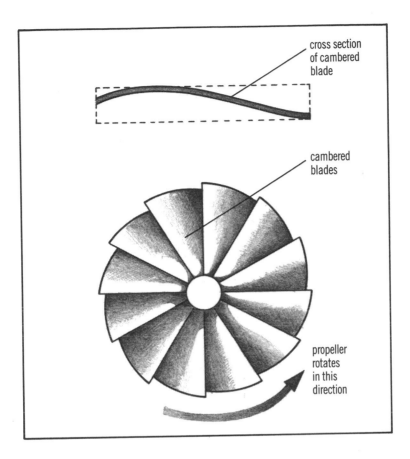

cross section
of cambered
blade

cambered
blades

propeller
rotates
in this
direction

**Figure 9. A propeller with a cambered blade.**

propeller using the same number of windings (and pulling the thread with the same force) each time. Do camber and smoothness affect performance? Experiment with the camber facing toward or away from the airstream. Is there a difference?

If you are interested in model airplanes, experiment with different propellers on the planes them-

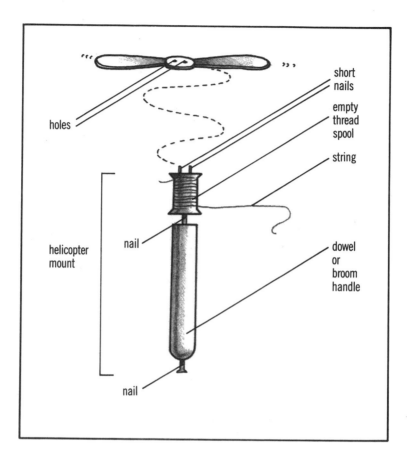

Figure 10. Launching a propeller.

selves. Use windup (rubber-band powered) models. Do this under adult supervision in case one of your designs throws the plane out of control.

**AUTOGYROS** • You can learn more about propellers by experimenting with autogyros. An autogyro is a propeller-driven aircraft supported by another propeller mounted on top of the body. This second propeller is air driven, not motor driven. The helicopter replaced the autogyro in general use.

You can make an autogyro by folding strips of paper 3¼ × 8¼ inches (8 × 21 cm), as shown in figure 11. Fold the strip in half lengthwise for 4 inches (10 cm) and cut along the fold to form the two wings. Fold these over so that they lie on opposite sides. Fold the base up to the midline, then make two triangular folds to the midline and your autogyro is ready.

**An autogyro from about 1940. Notice the two different types of propellers: the motor driven propeller in front, and the air driven propeller mounted on top of the body.**

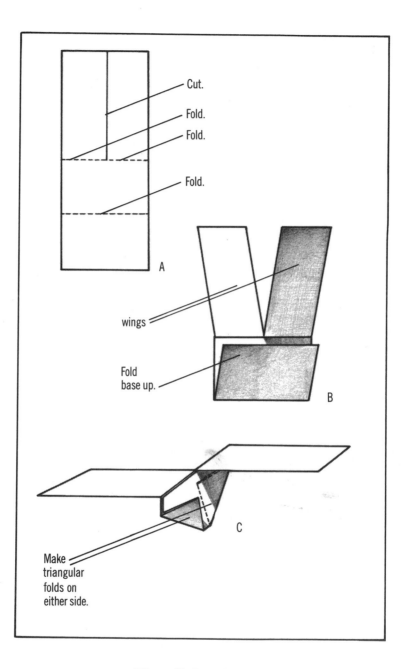

Cut.

Fold.

Fold.

Fold.

A

wings

Fold
base up.

B

C

Make
triangular
folds on
either side.

**Figure 11. An autogyro.**

Hold your autogyro as high as you can, and release it. Does anything slow the descent? What makes it spin? Working under adult supervision, release the autogyro from the upstairs window of a building. What happens?

Make two more autogyros the same as the first. In one of these, shorten the length by 1 inch (2.5 cm), in the other by 2 inches (5 cm). See figure 12. Release the three autogyros from the same height

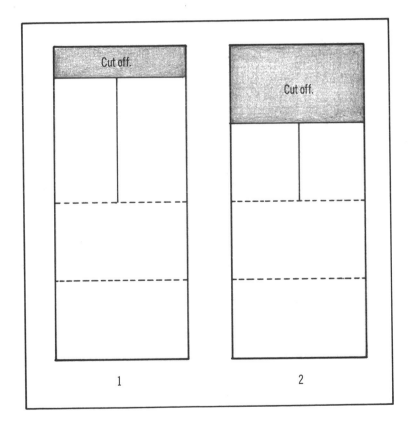

Figure 12. Two more autogyros.

and note the order in which they reach the ground. Are wing size, air resistance, and rate of descent related?

**JETS AND JET ENGINES** • We are all familiar with jet-propelled aircraft, which whisk people halfway around the world in a matter of hours. These aircraft date back to 1941 and were the outcome of research by a number of engineers, including Sir Frank Whittle, an Englishman. But the principle of the jet engine goes back to the seventeenth century when Sir Isaac Newton stated that for every action there is an equal and opposite reaction. In a jet engine, the escaping gases are the action; the reaction is the forward thrust.

A balloon is a simple jet engine. Blow up a small balloon, release it, and watch it dart across the room. What are the forces of action and reaction?

Hero of Alexandria is said to have built the first jet engine in the first century A.D. It consisted of a metal sphere mounted on a hollow axle. Steam under pressure from a boiler was fed into the axle and escaped from the side jets in such a way that the sphere rotated, as you can see in figure 13.

You can make a balloon jet that works similarly. Refer to figure 14. Obtain a long, sausage-shaped balloon, a cork that will fit snugly into the balloon nozzle, 12 inches (30 cm) of thread, 2 flexible straws, and rubber cement.

Drill two holes in the cork ⅛ to ³⁄₁₆ inch (3 to 4 mm) or big enough for the straws to fit through. Cut the straws ½ inch (13 mm) on either side of the flex,

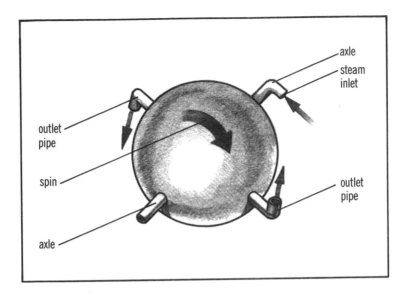

Figure 13. Hero's steam-powered jet,
built in the first century B.C.

bend each to form a right angle, pour on a little cement to hold firm at a right angle, and the jets are ready.

Glue the jets to the sides of the cork, jets pointed in opposite directions. Then glue one end of the thread to the center of the closed end of the cork. As soon as the glue has dried, blow up the balloon, pinch the neck with your fingers, slip the cork into the nozzle, and hold the end of the thread. Let go of the neck. What happens? Why?

Balloon jets utilize air pressure, but real jets burn fuel. You can make a simple fuel-burning jet from common materials.

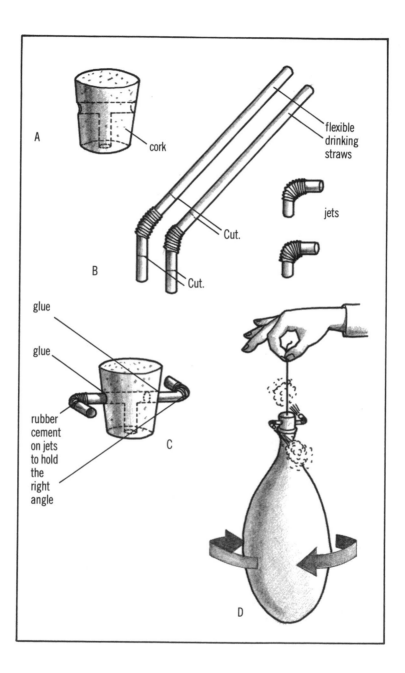

**Figure 14. A balloon jet engine.**

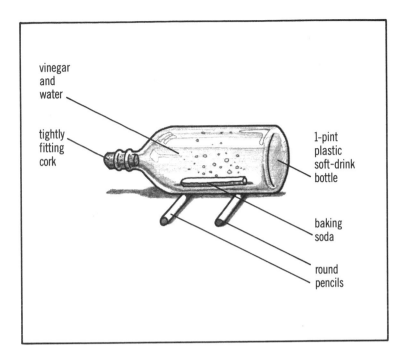

vinegar
and
water

tightly
fitting
cork

1-pint
plastic
soft-drink
bottle

baking
soda

round
pencils

**Figure 15. Demonstrating thrust.**

THE EXHAUST FROM YOUR JET WILL BE MESSY, SO DO THIS EXPERIMENT OUTDOORS AND WITH AN ADULT'S HELP. Place two pencils a few inches apart on a smooth, level surface. Put 2 teaspoons of baking soda onto a piece of paper and roll the paper into a tube thin enough to slip into a 1-pint (1.5-liter) plastic soft-drink bottle. Fill the bottle three-fourths full with a mixture containing half vinegar and half water.

Quickly put the paper tube into the bottle, cork the bottle, then place it on the pencils. The setup should look like the one in figure 15. Point the cork away from yourself and others in the area, as it will fly away as the gas pressure inside the bottle increases. Don't stand too close to the bottle or you will get vinegar all over yourself. Don't stand in the path of the bottle either. What happens inside the bottle? What happens to the bottle?

**HOW BIRDS FLY** • Try to obtain different types of feathers. Sort them into piles according to use—flight, insulation, etc. Look at a flight feather carefully. What qualities make it light and strong?

Closeup of a flight feather of a hawk (top)
and insulating feathers (below)

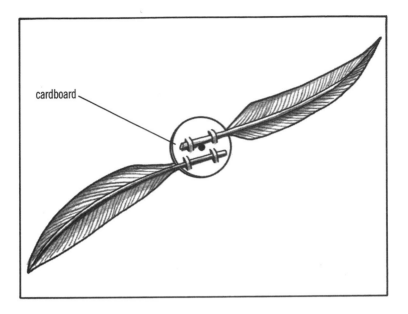

**Figure 16. A feather propeller.**

Find out how zip-fasteners are used in wing feathers. Split the web of a feather, draw your fingers lightly over the break, and note what happens. Is this what birds do when they preen themselves? Does preening help birds fly?

The wingtip feathers of birds act like propellers in a figure **8**, which moves the bird forward, and the movement of the airstream over the inner part of the wing produces lift.

You can make your own feather propellers. Choose two good wingtip feathers, cut a small circle of cardboard, and attach the feathers as shown in figure 16. Test your propeller outside.

**OUTDOOR OBSERVATIONS** • Watch gulls or hawks taking to the air. Do the wingtips move more than the inner part of the wing? Do they seem to be acting as propellers?

Are all birds streamlined? How is the tail spread or closed with speed? What do birds do with their legs during flight? Compare this with what a pilot does with the landing gear of an aircraft during takeoff.

Observe insects and, if you can, study their wings under a magnifying glass.

Try to view a film on squid or octopuses swimming. How do they move? Find out whether they are "jet propelled."

If you are near a pond or stream, watch water spiders, tadpoles, and frogs. Find other types of animals whose shape and movement you can observe. Would you feel convinced now that there is a connection between shape and speed? Perhaps streamlining is not always beneficial to an animal. Do unstreamlined animals have any advantages over streamlined ones?

# STABILITY, SAFETY, AND CONTROL

When you pick up a long piece of wood or pipe you will probably hold it in the middle instead of near one end. Somehow you know that carrying the object this way is easier. What you might not know is that each time you do this you are finding the *center of gravity* (COG) of the object.

The center of gravity is the point in an object where the entire mass of the object seems to be concentrated. A force acting upward at this point equal to the weight of the object would support the object. The object would be stable. It would balance.

For example, a tight-rope walker can balance on a tightrope provided his COG is exactly above the rope.

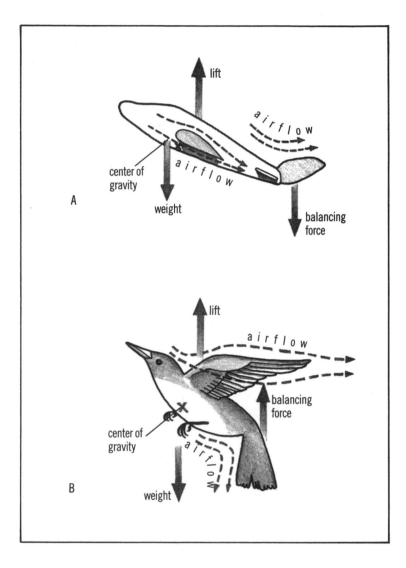

**Figure 17. Balancing in flight. If the center of gravity is in the wrong place, the aircraft or bird could topple. In both examples, the tail is used for balancing.**

The ruler on your desk will balance on a pin provided you find the exact balance point. The tightrope walker and the ruler will both topple over if they are not centered over the balance point. Try walking on one of the balance rails in a playground. What happens when you move your arms around? Hold a weight in one hand. What happens to your balance?

To ensure stability, airplanes are designed with the COG in mind (see figure 17). Keeping the weight forward and low keeps aircraft from toppling sideways, pitching, and nose-diving. The tail also prevents pitching and nose-diving. Swept-back wings and dihedral wings—angled upward so that both wings form a V—also help balance an aircraft. And finally, forward movement contributes toward balance.

**COG INVESTIGATIONS** • Construct the setup shown in figure 18. Try to get the objects to balance.

Do you think the COG is in the same place in every plane, or does it depend on the placement of the cargo, passengers, and engines? You might want to investigate the COGs of balsa-wood gliders and engine-powered model airplanes. Are the COGs in different places on these planes? Which planes seem to fly the best? have the most stability? climb the best? do the best maneuvers? BE CAREFUL WHEN OBSERVING FLYING MODEL PLANES.

**SPEED AND BALANCE** • Speed helps in balancing. Movement keeps you from falling off your bicycle and

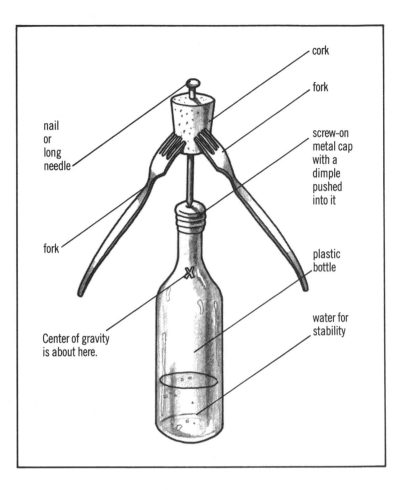

cork

fork

nail
or
long
needle

screw-on
metal cap
with a
dimple
pushed
into it

fork

plastic
bottle

Center of gravity
is about here.

water for
stability

**Figure 18. Balancing a cork
and two forks on a nail.**

keeps a bird from falling to earth. An albatross or
gull or glider soars into the wind and is lifted by the
wind to a great height. Then the bird or glider turns
and dives with the wind to gain speed. This keeps it
going as it turns into the wind and climbs again, rather

like a spinning coin. A slow-spinning coin will wobble and quickly fall over, but a fast-spinning coin will spin smoothly and only wobble when it slows down. The same happens with a top, a Frisbee, and a spinning card.

Try spinning some objects like coins, Frisbees, hoops, tops, and cards. What do you observe? Are you more stable on your bicycle when you are moving quickly or slowly? When you walk the rail in the playground, do you balance better when going slowly or more quickly?

**KITES** • You can investigate stability using kites. Use commercial kites or make your own from light cardboard, paper, plastic, or wood. Experiment with tails and different shapes. How does a tail help a kite? Does it correspond to any part of an airplane?

To build your own kite, cut a sheet of light, strong plastic (for example, a cut-apart garbage bag) approximately 2½ × 4 feet (0.8 × 1.2 m). In the center, cut out a circle 12 inches (30 cm) in diameter. Attach two pieces of ³⁄₁₆-inch (5-mm) dowel to the plastic sheet with strong adhesive tape. Refer to figure 19. Attach string or nylon thread to the sheet with the same tape, tie as shown in the figure, and your kite is ready to try.

Experiment with larger and smaller sheets of plastic and vary the size of the hole. Which kite performs best? flies the highest? is the most stable?

**BIRDS AND INSECTS** • Birds fly according to the same principles of flight as airplanes, but a bird's wings have to provide forward motion in addition to lift.

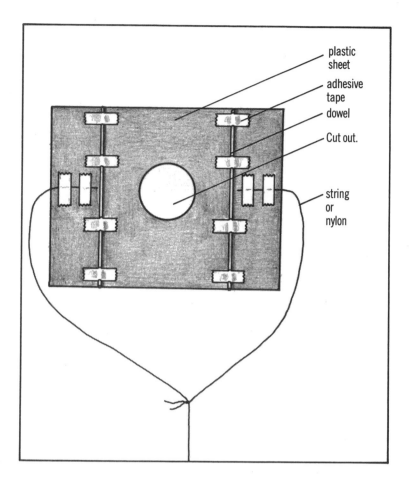

**Figure 19. An experimental kite.**

The wing is a modified five-fingered limb with the wrist and hand bones reduced and only the second finger well formed. The thumb is separate and has its own fingers.

DO THE FOLLOWING ONLY UNDER GUIDANCE OF A TRAINED NATURALIST, SO THAT YOU WON'T

HURT THE BIRD. If you can't get to a nature center or zoo, do some extra reading on birds in flight.

Have the naturalist hold a bird so that you can look along the front edge of the wing and find the small thumb wing, which should be halfway along the wing (see figure 20). You may be able to lift this from the main wing (carefully). In soaring birds such as hawks, the thumb wing opens at slow speeds. This helps stabilize the bird. Also look for the shoulder wingtip feathers. At slow speeds these separate, allowing air to spill through so that the bird does not stall in flight.

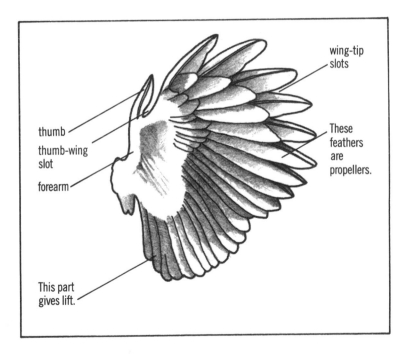

**Figure 20. A bird's wing.**

An artist's rendering of an F-111A, showing three wing positions which can be used by the pilot, depending upon whether the airplane is taking off or landing, in flight at moderate speed, or flying at supersonic speed.

Find out what devices airplanes have to prevent stalling at slow speeds.

Catch a fly. Use a magnifying glass to look for the balancers or halteres (clublike organs) behind the wings. These structures help with balance. A fly cannot balance if these are removed. See if you can find out exactly how these work.

**OBSERVING BIRDS AND AIRCRAFT ●** Does the body lie below the wings in all birds? If so, what is the advantage to this design? Which birds fly by flapping their small wings quickly, then folding them to their sides? Which birds have large wings and soar like sailplanes?

Watch birds as they change direction in flight. Do they steer with their wings or their tails? How do birds use their tails for braking and control? Watch ducks land on water.

Also watch gulls landing. Do they spread their wingtip feathers? If so, why? Which birds glide with sweptback wings? Look at pictures of jets in books or at airports or museums. Which ones have the most sweptback wings? How do the wings slant in a modern jet transport plane?

Some aircraft, such as the General Dynamics F-111A, can change during flight from a straight wing (best for takeoffs and landings) to a sweptback wing (breaking the sound barrier and supersonic flight).

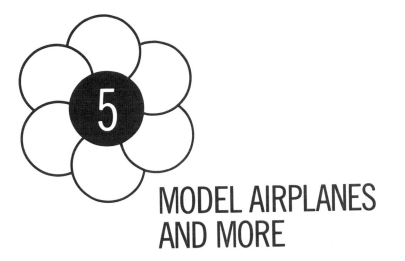

# MODEL AIRPLANES
# AND MORE

You can learn more about the principles of flight by building your own flying machines. Try the projects in this chapter for building gliders, parachutes, and hovercraft and then try designing your own aircraft. If you build the wind gauge and airspeed indicators also described, you will add to your knowledge in ways you perhaps never thought about. And by building the wind tunnel you will be building a tool to help you design and test your own designs.

To get ideas for new types of wings, propellers, parachutes, balloons, and other craft, you may want to look in some of the books listed in the bibliography.

**GLIDERS** • One of the most primitive flying devices is the glider. A glider is heavier than air. Since it has no engine, it has to rely on air currents to keep it airborne. Early gliders were launched from hilltops in order to develop enough speed to create sufficient lift to defy gravity.

A glider sails on a hill of air drawn forward and downward. Just as a bird with outstretched wings locates and soars upward on a rising current of air, so too does a pilot in a glider. The lift of the bird's wing and of the glider's, plus the upthrust of the air, keep both the bird and the glider aloft for hours with neither wing movement nor engine propulsion.

A SIMPLE GLIDER ○ Take a sheet of 8-½ × 11-inch (21.5 × 27.5-cm) writing paper, stand on a chair, holding the paper high above your head, then release it. Note its movement.

Now make three ¼-inch (6-mm) folds along the front edge of the sheet, as shown in figure 21. Release as before and note what happens.

Do the two "gliders" fly differently? Do you know why?

THE PARAGLIDER ○ The paraglider (also called a Ragallo wing) resembles a kite, and on launching cuts smoothly through the air.

Refer to figure 22 when making your glider.

1. Fold a sheet of 8½ × 11-inch (21.5 × 27.5-cm) paper lengthwise. Crease it down the middle; then unfold it flat on a desk or table.

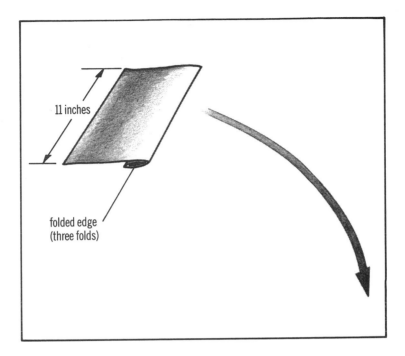

11 inches

folded edge
(three folds)

Figure 21. A simple glider.

2. Make three successive triangular folds to the center.

3. Open and tape the loose ends. Flex until the plane assumes the shape shown.
    Launch the glider.

You can also make a large Ragallo wing from a sheet of drawing paper whose dimensions are 18 × 25 inches (45 × 63 cm).
    Compare the handling of the two gliders. Which flies faster? farther? higher? launches more

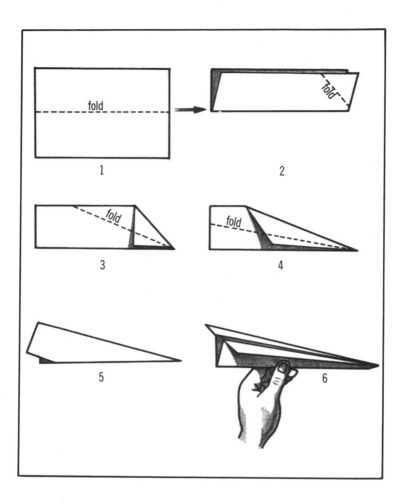

Figure 22. Making a paraglider.

smoothly? Try loop-the-loops by aiming down when you launch. Which performs better?

Experiment with different weights of paper and different materials, different-shaped wings, big wings and small wings, large bodies, paper clip weights added to the nose, and so on.

**PARACHUTES** • Parachutes slow down moving people and objects. Jet-fighter pilots wear them in case they have to leave their plane in midair. The old space capsules like the Mercury, Gemini, and Apollo had them to slow their descent through the atmosphere from space. Drag racers use parachutes attached to the back of their cars to slow them down after they have crossed the finish line.

A parachute jumper. As the parachute descends, it drives air out of its way. The air pushing back on the parachute slows the moving object attached to the parachute.

A moving parachute drives air out of its way. The air pushing back on the parachute slows the moving object attached to the parachute.

You can watch how a parachute works by tossing a folded handkerchief into the air and watching it descend.

You can make your own parachute using a piece of cloth or a sturdy paper napkin. Unfold the napkin all the way. Cut four pieces of light string a foot (30 cm) long. Glue or tape one end of each piece of string to a corner of the napkin. Attach a small weight to the other end of the lengths of string. (Try a piece of modeling clay, a small fishing sinker, a small stone, etc.) Under adult supervision, drop the parachute from a window or the top of a staircase, or carefully compress the parachute and weight combination and toss it into the air. Be careful not to hurt anyone when you launch your parachute.

Experiment with different materials and sizes.

**DETECTING AIR CURRENTS** • Pilots rely on wind gauges to tell them the speed and direction of the wind. You can make a simple device that detects air movement from a feather, wire, thimble, glue, a pin, modeling clay, and wood. Assemble your materials as shown in figure 23. Attach the thimble to the feather with tape or glue. Add wire to the tip of the feather as shown until it balances perfectly on the pin head.

Put the detector on the table and walk quietly by it. Does the feather move? Open and shut a nearby door. What happens to the feather? Watch the feather in a "still" room and decide if the air in the room is really still.

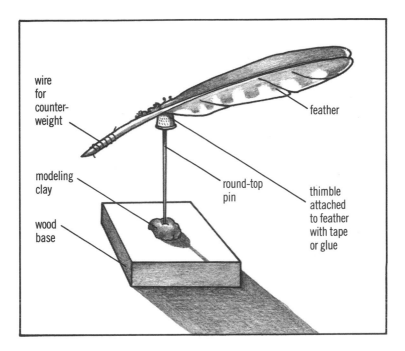

wire
for
counter-
weight

feather

modeling
clay

round-top
pin

thimble
attached
to feather
with tape
or glue

wood
base

Figure 23. An air movement detector.

**MEASURING AIRSPEED** • Pilots need to know how fast they are flying at all stages of flight, from takeoff to landing. For example, they can't leave the ground until they are going fast enough, and they can't land until they have slowed to a certain speed. Speed is shown on the airspeed indicator.

The airspeed indicator system determines airspeed by measuring pressure differences in two tubes into which air rushes when the plane is in motion. The faster the plane, the lower the pressure in one tube and the farther to the right the needle on the gauge moves.

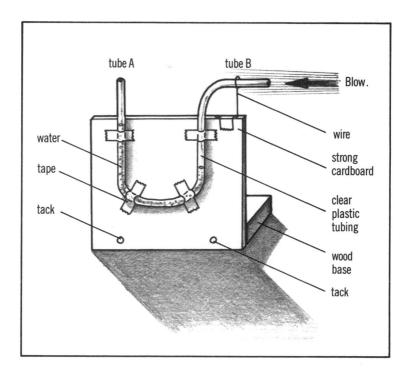

**Figure 24. An aircraft airspeed indicator.**

Building your own simple airspeed indicator will help you understand what is happening.

Cut one piece of clear plastic tubing about 18 inches (45 cm) long and arrange it as shown in figure 24. Fix the tube in place with cellophane tape or with wire. Add water to the straight end of the tube until there is a 3-inch (8-cm) column of water in each arm of the tube.

Blow hard across the tube so that the airstream strikes open end *B* and passes over open end *A*, as shown in the figure. What happens to the water level in the tube?

Now blow more gently onto the tube. What happens to the water level now?

Remember some of your experiments with lift? Remember how a moving airstream lowers the pressure above a wing, lifting the wing? Do you suppose that this is what is happening in the tube?

If you could hook up a speedometer-type gauge to the tube, would the needle be farther to the right (the "faster" end) when you blew hard or when you blew softly?

**WIND TUNNELS** • Before an aircraft design is finalized and a plane put into production, models are tested in a wind tunnel. A wind tunnel is a specially built tunnel-shaped chamber through which air is forced at a variety of speeds. By measuring the airflow patterns over the wings and body, engineers can tell how the plane will behave in flight. Engineers can test different wing and body designs to find the best ones for the plane they need to build.

You can do some testing of your own if you have your own wind tunnel. Here's one design. Refer to figure 25 when putting it together.

In a cardboard box about 10 × 10 × 20 inches (25 × 25 × 50 cm), neatly cut out a large window in one side, leaving about 1 inch of cardboard around the windows for support. Tape clear plastic sheeting over the window. Make large windows in both ends of the box, too.

Using a model airplane that is smaller than the box, drill a hole on the underside of its body, insert a strong piece of wire into the hole, and fix in place with rubber cement. Any inexpensive balsa-wood or

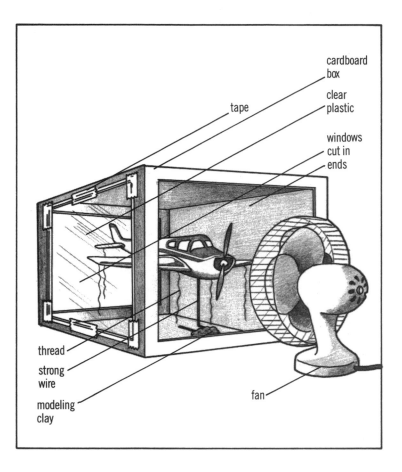

cardboard
box

clear
plastic

windows
cut in
ends

tape

thread

strong
wire

modeling
clay

fan

**Figure 25. A wind tunnel.**

cardboard model airplane will do, or you can build your own. Attach the other end of the wire to the base of the box with modeling clay.

Cut eight 6-inch (15-cm) pieces of black thread and attach these with cellophane tape to different places on the airplane, for example, the wings, fuselage, and rudder.

HAVE AN ADULT SET UP A SMALL FAN SO THAT IT FACES THE MODEL. The safest fans are the little plastic table fans with a cage around the blades. Turn on the fan and observe the threads. If the fan has different speeds, try them out and look for any differences in the patterns of the threads.

Smoke can be used to show airstreams. DESIGN A SAFE EXPERIMENT USING SMOKE IN YOUR WIND TUNNEL. BE SURE TO WORK UNDER ADULT SUPERVISION.

Do some reading on Schlieren photography. How does this type of photography help flight engineers?

**HOVERCRAFTS** • A hovercraft is a device that literally moves on a cushion of air. The engines of the hovercraft compress air, then release it through vents in the base of the device. As a result, the entire machine rests—or hovers—on air. Because friction is reduced to a minimum, the hovercraft is easily propelled by allowing air under pressure to escape through jets at the rear, front, or sides of the device. Movement is possible in any direction. Wear and tear are reduced to a minimum.

To explore the principle of the hovercraft, you can make a low-friction air puck. DO THIS WITH ADULT SUPERVISION.

Cut a circular piece of ⅛-inch (3-mm) thick hardboard, stiff cardboard, or plywood 4 to 5 inches (10 to 12 cm) in diameter.

Drill a ¹⁄₁₀-inch (2.5-mm) hole in the center of the disk. Glue a thread spool to the disk so that the

A U.S. Navy hovercraft. The engines of the hovercraft compress air, then release it through vents in the base of the craft, causing it to rest on a cushion of air. The craft can then be propelled by allowing air under pressure to escape through jets at the rear, front, or sides.

hole in the spool exactly matches the hole in the disk. Coat the glue over the entire end of the spool, leaving no gaps for air to leak through. Wait for the glue to dry. See figure 26.

Now inflate a balloon and twist the neck of the balloon to hold the air in as you slip the end of the balloon over the end of the spool. Release the balloon, making sure it untwists. You will hear the hiss of escaping air and should see your air puck resting on a cushion of air. Make sure you choose a very flat, level, smooth surface for this. Give the edge of the

disk a light flick. What happens? Will the puck hover over water? Figure out a way to add a second balloon that will move the puck horizontally.

Here are plans for another hovercraft. AGAIN, BE SURE TO WORK UNDER ADULT SUPERVISION.

Obtain a large, solid piece of polystyrene scrap (or stick polystyrene bricks together). Use a sharp knife (CAREFUL!) to cut out a boat 12 to 15 inches

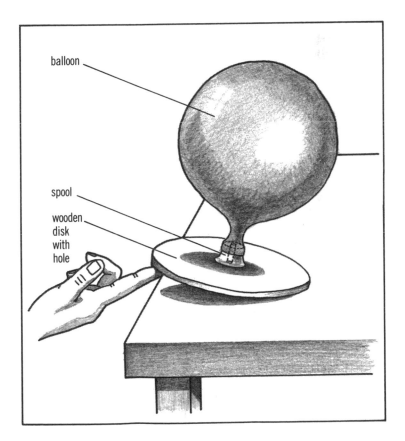

**Figure 26. A low-friction air puck.**

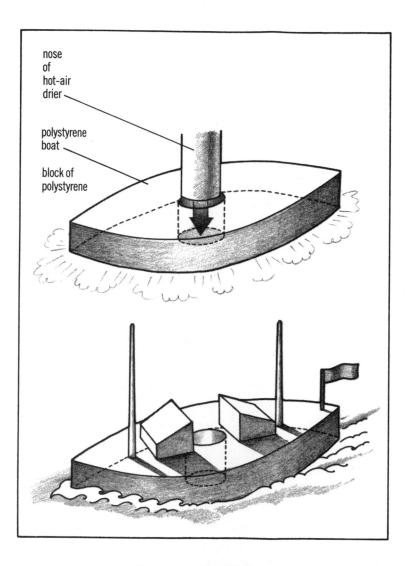

**Figure 27. A hoverboat.**

(about 30 to 40 cm) long, 3 inches (8 cm) deep, and 4 inches (10 cm) wide at the middle. Cut a hole in the center 2 inches (5 cm) in diameter or large enough to take the nose of a small hair dryer. You may have

to experiment with the size of your boat in order to get it to hover properly. Place the boat on a flat surface. See figure 27.

You are now ready to try out your hovercraft. Switch on the hair dryer (put the dryer on a cold setting if it has one) and hold the nose just over the central opening without touching the boat. You should see the boat resting on a cushion of air. Whichever way you move the dryer the boat should follow. If the dryer has no cold air setting, be careful not to let the boat heat up too much or the plastic will melt.

You may want to build one last hovercraft.

To do this you will need a vacuum cleaner with a hose and a blowout attachment. Obtain a small-

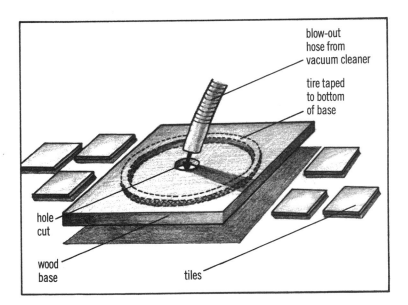

**Figure 28. A hovercraft made from a bicycle tire.**

diameter bicycle or motorcycle tire and cut a square of ¼-inch (6-mm) plywood, masonite, or chipboard just big enough to cover it. Tape the tire to the bottom of the plywood. At the center of the wood, cut or drill a hole large enough to take the hose of the vacuum cleaner. Have some weights like light books or floor tiles on hand (available at building-supply stores at reasonable prices). See figure 28.

Start the vacuum cleaner and place the nozzle through the hole. What happens? Now add a tile to each side of the wood base. What happens now? Add more tiles, one at a time. What happens eventually?

**OUTDOOR OBSERVATIONS WITH PLANTS** • Did you ever see dandelion seeds rise into the air, carried by puffs of wind? What happens when the seeds fall to earth? They come down delicately. The dandelion seed is carried aloft and brought to earth by the same fluffy parachute. The ability to use the wind allows the dandelion plant to spread its seeds far from the parent plant.

Look for similar plants, for example, cotton grass, milkweed, and thistles. Examine their seeds along with the seeds of the dandelion under a magnifying glass or, if you have one, a microscope. Look also for winged seeds of trees such as maples and sycamores. What happens when you drop these seeds from a height?

Pollen from flowers also spread on the wind, but without fluff. What plants and trees are pollinated by the wind? Read about the way that mushrooms and other fungi spread their spores.

# BALLOONS

Balloons, blimps, and dirigibles are different forms of lighter-than-air airships. All defy the force of gravity because they are filled with hot air or with a gas that is lighter than air. A hot-air balloon works on the principle that hot air rises. An on-board burner heats the air in the balloon, expanding it and making it lighter than the cooler air outside. When the air inside the balloon is warm enough, the balloon takes off.

Airships filled with a gas lighter than air once used hydrogen, because hydrogen is the lightest gas in the universe. The problem with hydrogen is that it is extremely inflammable. That means it catches fire easily and can explode as well. Today a mixture

**This U.S. Navy blimp had hooks on the side where small airplanes could be attached.**

of helium and other gases is used in many blimps and balloons. You probably have bought a foil balloon at a fair. It probably contained some helium.

Dirigibles, blimps, and balloons differ in construction. Blimps and balloons are nonrigid airships. Their shape is maintained by the pressure of the gases inside the envelope. Dirigibles are rigid airships. Their body consists of fabric covering a rigid frame.

Small balloons are operated by one person, while larger craft have a larger crew. Crew and passengers usually ride in some sort of basket suspended from the bottom of the balloon. Weather balloons and other specialized balloons carry equipment only.

The early history of balloons goes back to 1513 when Leonardo da Vinci is said to have filled very thin wax figures with hot air and made them fly. In 1670 Francisco de Lana drew and described a lighter-than-air craft. He also described an air raid carried out by a balloon ship. Four airless copper spheres were designed to lift the craft, but he failed to realize that air pressure would crush the thin globes.

A small hot-air balloon was developed in the eighteenth century, but the first large balloon wasn't flown until 1783. This was a smoke-filled balloon made by the Montgolfier brothers in France. The first manned flight took place later in the same year, also in France.

A balloon will climb until the weight of the balloon, the gas, and the load equal the weight of the air displaced. The balloon is then in a state of balance or equilibrium. Should the crew wish to climb higher, weights called ballast (often sand) are dropped. To land the balloon, gas is released until the balloon loses the ability to counteract the force of gravity.

What happens when you release a balloon outside and it rises? Will it explode or implode (or neither)? Will it stay up forever or eventually return to earth? You might want to check your guess by flying a balloon on a piece of string the way you would fly a kite.

A contemporary depiction of the 1783
launching of the Montgolfier brothers'
smoke-filled balloon over Paris, France

**MAKING AND FLYING LIGHTER-THAN-AIR BALLOONS** • Since hot air balloons require large amounts of very hot air, they are potentially dangerous to experiment with in the home. Fortunately, you can demonstrate how hot air balloons work by using a "hot-water balloon," which will float in cooler water in the same way that a hot-air balloon floats in air.

To show this you need two small balloons and a tub of water at room temperature. Fill up one balloon with hot water. Be sure to get all the air out of the balloon and tie its neck in a knot. Drop the balloon in the tub. Does it sink or float? Now fill the second balloon with very cold water, and tie it off the same way. Drop it in the tub. What happens? What happens to the hot water balloon when it cools off?

**SELF-INFLATION** • Echo 1 and 2 were giant, aluminum-coated plastic balloons that inflated in space to about 100 feet (30 m) and were used as communications satellites.

You can demonstrate how a balloon self-inflates because of a change in pressure. Inflate a small balloon just slightly and tie off the neck with thread. Place the balloon in a clear bottle with a small opening. Put the bottle opening to your mouth and suck on the bottle to create low air pressure in the bottle. What happens to the small balloon inside the bottle?

How did the Echo satellites inflate in space?

**EXPANSION CAUSES COOLING** • The air inside an inflated balloon or tire is under pressure. An automobile tire might be inflated to a pressure of 32 pounds per square inch (227 kPa) and a racing-bicycle tire to as much as 90 or 100 pounds per square inch (620 to 690 kPa). The normal pressure of the atmosphere at sea level is only 15 pounds per square inch (103 kPa).

In a compressed gas, whether it's air, carbon dioxide, or helium, the molecules are pushed closer together than they are when the gas is not under as much pressure. As a result, the forces of attraction among molecules are greater. When pressurized gas is allowed to escape suddenly through a small opening in the container, the gas molecules fly apart from one another and the gas expands. To do this the molecules require additional energy to overcome the attractive force that once held them closer together. The energy used to accomplish this is the heat energy of the molecules themselves. In taking away heat from itself, the temperature of the gas drops.

You can demonstrate this cooling effect by experimenting with a bicycle tire or any kind of inner tube.

Unscrew the valve cap if there is one and make sure the valve has a "pin" in the middle (sometimes they are broken off). Take the air temperature using a plastic thermometer. Ask an adult to help you find a good, safe thermometer.

Now press down on the metal valve pin until the air begins to escape. Hold your fingers over the escaping air. Does it feel cold? Hold the thermometer in the stream of escaping air for a few seconds. Does the thermometer register a lower temperature? If so, how much lower? Does any water condense on the valve? If so, why? What happens if you hold the valve open until most of the air has escaped?

Now pump up the tire. Does the valve get hot? Does the tire feel warmer than when deflated? If you are using a lightweight bicycle pump, the kind that fits on the bicycle, does any part of the pump get hotter when you are pumping? Hold your finger over the hose or valve end of the pump and pump so that only a little air leaks out under your finger. Do you notice anything unusual about the air or the end of the pump?

When you blow up a balloon, do you think the air in the balloon is warmer, colder, or the same temperature as in your lungs? Does air temperature have anything to do with the fact that balloons you blow up are not lighter than air?

Investigate the methods scientists and engineers use to obtain superlow temperatures. How does a refrigerator work? The bibliography at the back of this book lists some sources to turn to for further information on some of these subjects.

**BALLOONS IN AIRSTREAMS** • You can easily investigate how a balloon behaves in a moving airstream. You will need a fan or portable hair dryer, a balloon, and thread. The safest fans are the little table models with the flexible blades inside a cage. If you use a different type of fan, be sure to work under adult supervision. If you use a hand-held hair dryer, use the cool-air setting.

Arrange the fan on a table so that it faces upward. Inflate a round balloon and tie off the neck with the thread, leaving a foot (30 cm) of thread dangling. Turn on the fan and place the balloon a about a yard (meter) above the fan or hair dryer. Hold the balloon steady with the thread if you have to by holding the thread near the fan or dryer. What happens to the balloon? Raise one side of the fan or dryer so that the airstream changes direction. Is there any change in the position or behavior of the balloon?

Take away the balloon and turn off the fan or dryer. Tie a short piece of thread to the end of the balloon. Bring the balloon into your kitchen or bathroom and turn on the cold water in the sink or bathtub. Hold the balloon in the stream of water by the thread. What happens? Try to pull the balloon away from the stream with the thread. Does the balloon behave differently from the way it did in the airstream?

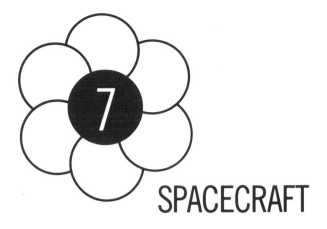

# SPACECRAFT

From the earliest times, the heavens have held a fascination for human beings. People have longed to reach out beyond our planet and probe the mysteries of the universe. Their speculations and discoveries have inspired the meditations of poets, artists, and philosophers and led to significant advances in astronomy and other sciences.

The idea of venturing into space is not new, nor is it confined to the twentieth century. In A.D. 160, for example, the Greek writer Lucian described a flight to the moon. The same theme was taken up in the late nineteenth century by the French writer Jules Verne in *A Trip to the Moon*.

Today, scientists and engineers have succeeded in overcoming the pull of gravity. They have sent manned and unmanned satellites into orbit around the earth, astronauts to the moon, and probes to the planets. Space exploration is adding tremendously to our knowledge and understanding of Earth and of the great universe beyond.

**THE ROCKET** • To reach into space, a vehicle had to be invented that could cope with the conditions found there. A conventional airplane wouldn't work, for two reasons. First, wings are useless because beyond a certain altitude the air is too thin to provide lift, and beyond the atmosphere there is no air at all. Second, there is insufficient oxygen in the atmosphere and no air in space for either a propeller or a jet engine to generate thrust. A propeller has to have air to push backward, and a jet won't burn when the air contains too little oxygen.

These problems were attacked by the two early pioneers of rocketry: Konstantin Tsiolkovsky, a Russian, and Robert Goddard, an American. In 1903 Tsiolkovsky wrote a book on space travel in which he described the use of liquid-fueled rockets. Goddard experimented with rockets between the two world wars. During World War II the Germans did most of the important work in rocketry.

It was recognized that a rocket did not need wings to fly, since maintaining lift was unnecessary. What was required was a lot of thrust and good stability. These were achieved in the basic design of the rocket.

**Robert Goddard, in 1926, stands beside the first successful liquid-fueled rocket.**

A rocket is a tube filled with fuel and closed at one end. When the fuel burns, gases are produced. Heat expands the gases, pushing them out the open end of the tube at high speed. Since every action has an equal and opposite reaction, the hot gases push against the closed end of the rocket. The rocket moves.

In his early experiments with rocket fuels, Dr. Goddard found that burning the fuel in air produced too little thrust, even at lower altitudes. (At higher altitudes there is even less oxygen, and eventually none at all.) More oxygen was needed to increase the burning rate. Today, many liquid-fueled rockets use liquid oxygen to burn hydrogen fuel.

**ROCKET PROPULSION** • To learn more about rockets, you can try the following experiments.

Set up the rocket model shown in figure 29. *A* is a wooden yard stick (meter stick). *B* is a string tied to the center of the stick. *C* is a cradle made of light cardboard or loose rubber bands to hold the balloon.

Blow up the balloon, *D*, and, holding the nozzle, put it in the cradle. Move the string tied to the stick to get balance; then release the nozzle. In which direction does the balloon move? the escaping air?

Experiment with a piece of thread to change the size of the balloon nozzle. Does the rate at which the air escapes affect the speed of the balloon rocket? Is this like a large rocket for launching a spacecraft?

**HEAVIER AND LIGHTER** • As a spacecraft rises above the earth, it is speeding up, or accelerating. For an as-

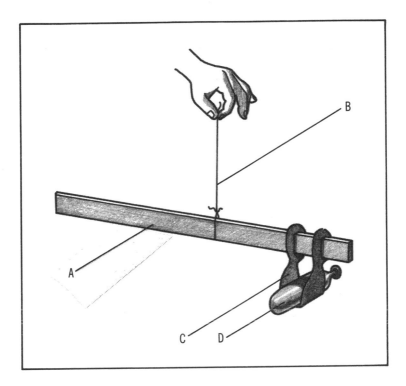

**Figure 29. Demonstrating rocket ship propulsion.**

tronaut to withstand the acceleration needed to put the spacecraft into orbit he or she lies down facing the line of flight. The astronaut lies in a form-fitting couch, and when the acceleration increases the body weight, the forces are distributed equally over nearly half the entire body surface. The astronaut remains quite comfortable despite the high acceleration stages of the flight. Does this compare with sitting in a car that suddenly accelerates or in a jet accelerating during takeoff?

Hang an iron nut or lead sinker by a very thin rubber band (cut in half to give a single strand) in a plastic peanut butter or jelly jar. Tie the upper end of the rubber band to a pencil. In the rest position, the pull of the rubber band will match the weight of the nut or sinker.

Now, holding the jar by its base, accelerate it rapidly upward. What happens to the rubber band? Accelerate the jar downward. Is the weight of the lead affected?

**INTO ORBIT** • Putting a spacecraft into orbit is like throwing a stone. It flies through the air, then falls back to earth. When you throw the stone harder, it flies farther through the air before the constant pull of gravity causes its path to curve back to earth. In orbital flight, the stone keeps curving downward but does not reach the earth. Rather it makes a great circle around the earth. It could keep going on like this forever, but if there is atmospheric drag, friction will slow it down. Then gravity takes over and pulls it back to earth.

Press a basketball or soccer ball firmly into a bucket. Cut a piece of stiff wire about 18 inches (45 cm) long from an unbent coathanger and bend the lower 6 inches (15 cm) into a loop. Bend the straight 12 inches (30 cm) of the wire upward so that it will stand straight up when the loop is flat on a flat surface. Tape the loop to the ball so that the straight end is upright over the center of the ball. Tie one end of a 20-inch (50-cm) piece of string to a metal weight (for example, a lead sinker), and tape the other end to a

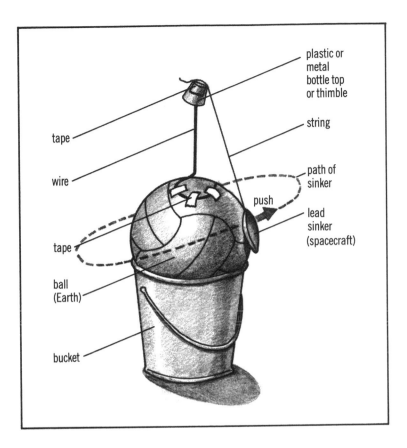

**Figure 30. Investigating spacecraft orbits.**

plastic bottle top. Adjust the string length so that the sinker rests on the side of the ball. See figure 30.

Give the sinker a light tap up and away from the ball. What happens? Now give it a tap to the side. How far does it travel before it falls back to the ball? Give the sinker a strong push forward so that its path takes it right around the ball. If the sinker represents a spacecraft and the ball the earth, what is the name for the sinker's path? Where is the near point (perigee) and the far point (apogee)? What factors cause a spacecraft to fall back to earth? What keeps a spacecraft on course? What is the shape of the orbit? Find out the name for such a curve.

**WEIGHTLESSNESS** • When a space capsule goes into orbit, the astronaut experiences weightlessness, the state when objects appear to have no weight. This occurs when the spacecraft is in earth orbit or falling freely around the earth. Gravity is pulling the spacecraft to earth; its speed carries it forward. As the spacecraft falls and at the same time moves forward, so also does the astronaut within. He or she acts toward the spacecraft as if he or she had no weight.

To investigate weightlessness, you will need a small doll supported by a thread in a small jar. You will also need two friends. When the thread is held by its upper end the doll is located in the center of the jar (see figure 31). Have one friend hold the thread in this way, stand (CAREFULLY!) on a desk or table and have your other friend stand on the floor below the jar. Have the friend holding the jar release it and have your other friend ready to catch it.

Both doll and jar fall under the influence of the same force—gravity. They will then both fall with the same acceleration. The doll (astronaut) will behave toward the container (spacecraft) as if it has no weight. Watch the jar closely while it is freefalling, concentrating on the doll.

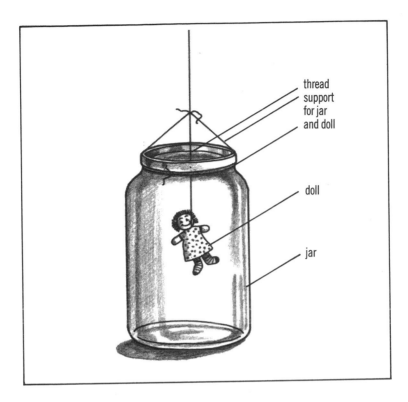

thread

support
for jar
and doll

doll

jar

Figure 31. Finding out about weightlessness.

**DECELERATION** • Much research has been undertaken to ensure the successful return of a spacecraft into the earth's atmosphere. Heating up caused by friction is a special problem, and materials have to be developed to withstand this re-entry heat. During re-entry, electrically charged air blocks out communications.

The astronauts' safety is also a major concern. The spacecraft is passing into the denser atmosphere at speeds up to 18,000 miles per hour (29,000 km/hr). Retro-rockets fire in the direction of the ship's travel to slow down the spacecraft, subjecting astronauts to forces up to eight times their body weight. The specially designed chairs help protect the astronauts.

To investigate these matters yourself, attach a shoebox to the top of a roller skate. Put a doll in the back end of the box and push the skate across the floor into a brick. What happens? Next, sit the doll with its back against the front end of the box and push the skate as before. What happens now? Does what happen here seem like what happens to an astronaut during reentry?

**REENTRY AND LANDING** • Before the days of the space shuttle, a spacecraft whose mission was complete was brought back to earth. Retro-rockets and parachutes slowed the craft's descent so that it made a gentle, or soft, landing.

To learn more about reentry and landing, you can do some experiments with balloons.

Attach a small weight—about ⅙ ounce (5 g) (a large paper clip will do)—to the closed end of a round balloon. Blow up the balloon and tie a small loop of thread around the nozzle to slow the escape of air. If the balloon falls immediately, use a lighter weight; if it takes off, add small pieces of modeling clay to the balloon, blow up the balloon, and try again. Keep experimenting until the balloon hangs in midair. (You may have to experiment with different sized loops of thread around the balloon nozzle to get the balloon in balance.) See figure 32.

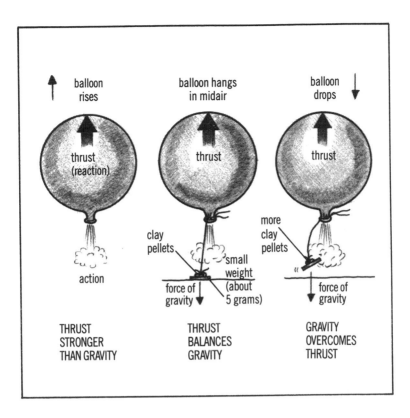

**Figure 32. Retro-rockets and soft landings.**

Blow up the balloon again and add an additional pellet or piece of clay. The pull of gravity will now exceed the thrust of the balloon by a small amount. Air gushing out the nozzle will brake the descent, and the balloon will "soft land." You may want to use art materials to simulate the features of the landscape of earth, the moon, or one of the other planets or their moons to land your spacecraft on. Look in an astronomy book for photographs or artist's renditions of these landscapes.

# FOR FURTHER READING

Cawthorne, Nigel. *Airliner.* London: Gloucester Press, 1988. A problem-solving approach to the different options of aircraft development.

Cromer, Richard. *The Miracle of Flight.* New York: Doubleday, 1968. Explains the aerodynamics of flight and how the physical structure and physiological processes of birds enable them to fly.

Dallison, Ken. *When Zeppelins Flew.* New York: Time-Life Books, 1969. A nicely illustrated history of Zeppelins, their inventor, and what it was like to fly in one. Includes cutaway of the *Graf Zeppelin.*

DiCerto, Joseph. *From Earth to Infinity: A Guide to Space Travel.* New York: Julian Messner, 1980. Comprehensive look at space travel, including explanation of rocket engine designs, from early rockets to the most recent.

Dwiggins, Don. *Riders of the Winds: The Story of Ballooning.* New York: Hawthorn Books, 1973. History of ballooning from the early experiments of the Montgolfiers in 1783 to the present.

Furniss, Tim. *Space.* New York: Franklin Watts, 1985. A close look at what's going on in the stratosphere: life support systems, communications to Earth, independent power generation, and rocket jets for maintaining orbit. Includes a cutaway of a liquid fuel rocket engine.

Gunston, Bill. *Aircraft.* New York: Franklin Watts, 1987. Explores the latest developments and future possibilities of aircraft technology.

Lampton, Christopher. *Rocketry: From Goddard to Space Travel.* New York: Franklin Watts, 1988. History of rocketry, focusing on the contributions of such pioneers as Tsiolkovsky, Goddard, and Von Braun.

Maynard, Chris, and Paton, John. *The History of Aircraft.* New York: Franklin Watts, 1982. Traces the history of manned flight from the first attempts to the present.

Percefull, Aaron W. *Balloons, Zeppelins, and Dirigibles.* New York: Franklin Watts, 1983. Flying without wings is explored, from the earliest hot air balloons to the *Graf Zeppelin*, as well as the uses of balloons, in war, exploration, sports, and recreation.

Simon, Hilda. *Feathers Plain and Fancy*. New York: Viking, 1969. All about bird feathers, different types, functions, etc.

Simon, Seymour. *The Great Paper Airplane Book*. New York: Puffin Books, 1971. Explains the science of flight, and shows how to design and make a variety of paper airplanes.

Stensbol, Ottar. *Model Flying Handbook*. New York: Sterling, 1979. Handbook for the hobbyist. Explains different types of models, how to build them, materials needed. Includes free-flying models, line controlled models, radio-controlled models. Good introduction to aerodynamics.

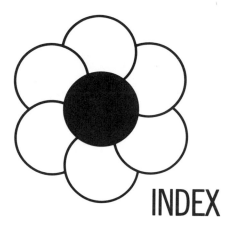

# INDEX

*Italic numbers indicate illustrations.*

EDUCATION